RUMPTOONS, the Donald J. Trump Presidency in Weekly Cartoons, 2016 – 2021

Copyright © 2021 by Martín Paredes
All rights reserved.

martinparedes.com

No part of this book may be reproduced in whole or in part without written permission from the publisher, except by reviewers who may quote brief excerpts in connection with a review in a newspaper, magazine, or electronic, mechanical, photocopying, recording, or other, without written permission from the publisher.

ISBN: 978-0-9884113-1-9

Illustrations: Martín Paredes
Author: Martín Paredes
Contributors:
                 Laura Gibson
                 Landon Gibson

El Paso News, Inc.
P.O. Box 536421
Orlando, FL 32853

elpasonewsinc.com

FORWARD

When Donald Trump came down the escalator on June 16, 2015 and proclaimed that Mexicans were "rapists," my thought was there we go again, blaming Mexicans and immigrants for the problems of the country. I wasn't surprised that Mexicans were now part of the national debate. I wasn't surprised that a presidential candidate denigrated Mexicans. There is always a bad apple in the bunch.

I just never thought that Donald Trump would be elected.

I understood that there are Americans who blame Mexicans for the country problems. I understood that immigrants were the boogeyman for the country's problems. What I did not believe was that there were enough American voters willing to elect Donald Trump.

As soon as Donald Trump was elected, I realized that I needed to do something. I needed a release for the reality that there were many Americans who wanted people like me ejected from the country. I needed to poke fun at the caricature that is Donald J. Trump to weather the horror that I knew was coming to people like me.

RUMPTOONS was born.

As I went about planning the weekly cartoon series, I considered that there was still some sanity left in the country forcing me to ask myself whether I would have enough material to produce a weekly cartoon about the disaster that is Donald Trump.

Shockingly there were several weeks where I had to choose the worst of several Trump disasters to cartoon for that week.

On January 17, 2021 I published my last **RUMPTOONS** cartoon - number 220.

The angst of living through the Trump presidency was somewhat released through these cartoons. Although Donald J. Trump provided me much material to work with, it was my family - Laura and Landon who provided me with much help in not only surviving the four years of Trump hell, but by making suggestions about what to cartoon each week.

This body of work would not have been possible without Laura and Landon not only because they showed me each day what real Americans are like, but because their support, encouragement and ideas helped create these cartoons.

Much of their ideas and suggestions are present in these pages. I am forever grateful for their love and support.

Now that we are moving forward under the Joe Biden administration it is my hope that Americans come to realize that the experiment of Donald J. Trump was an utter failure, especially his war on minorities, people of color and immigrants.

Martín Paredes
January 20, 2021

THE DONALD J TRUMP PRESIDENCY IN WEEKLY CARTOONS 2016 - 2021

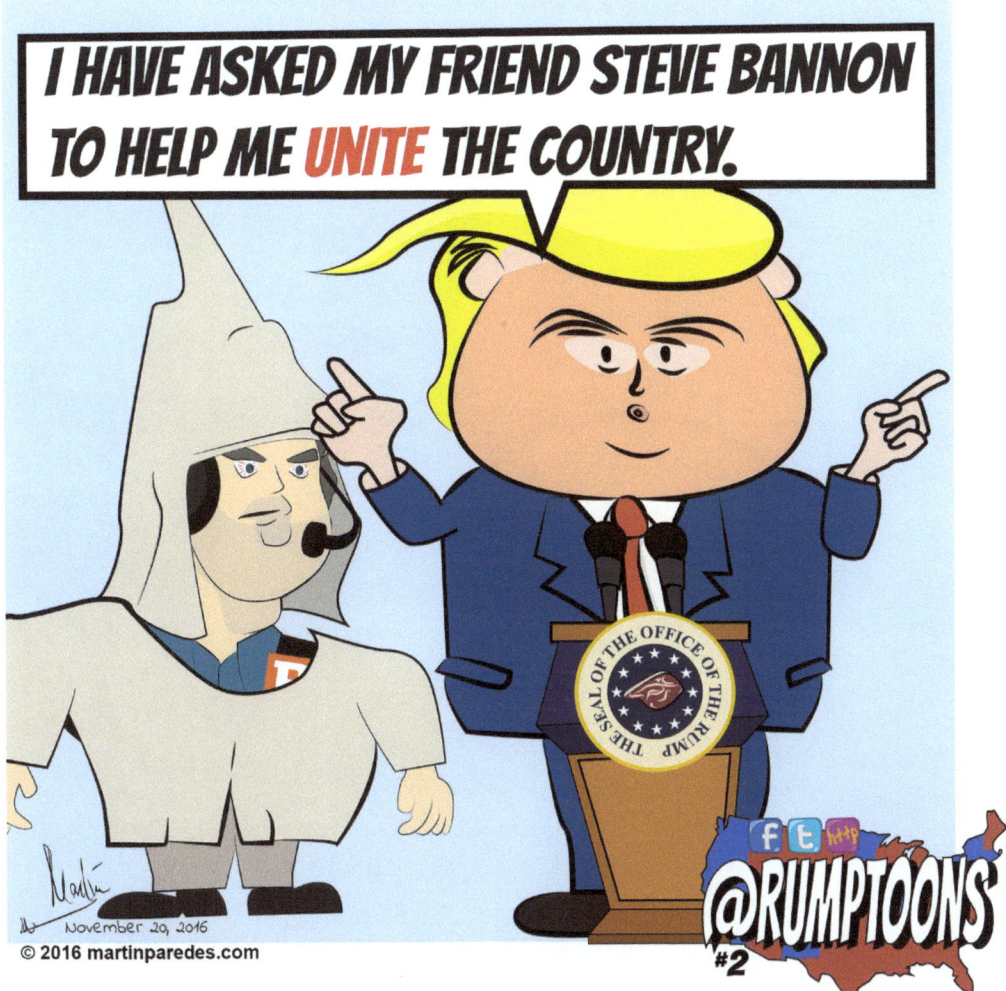

RUMPTOONS

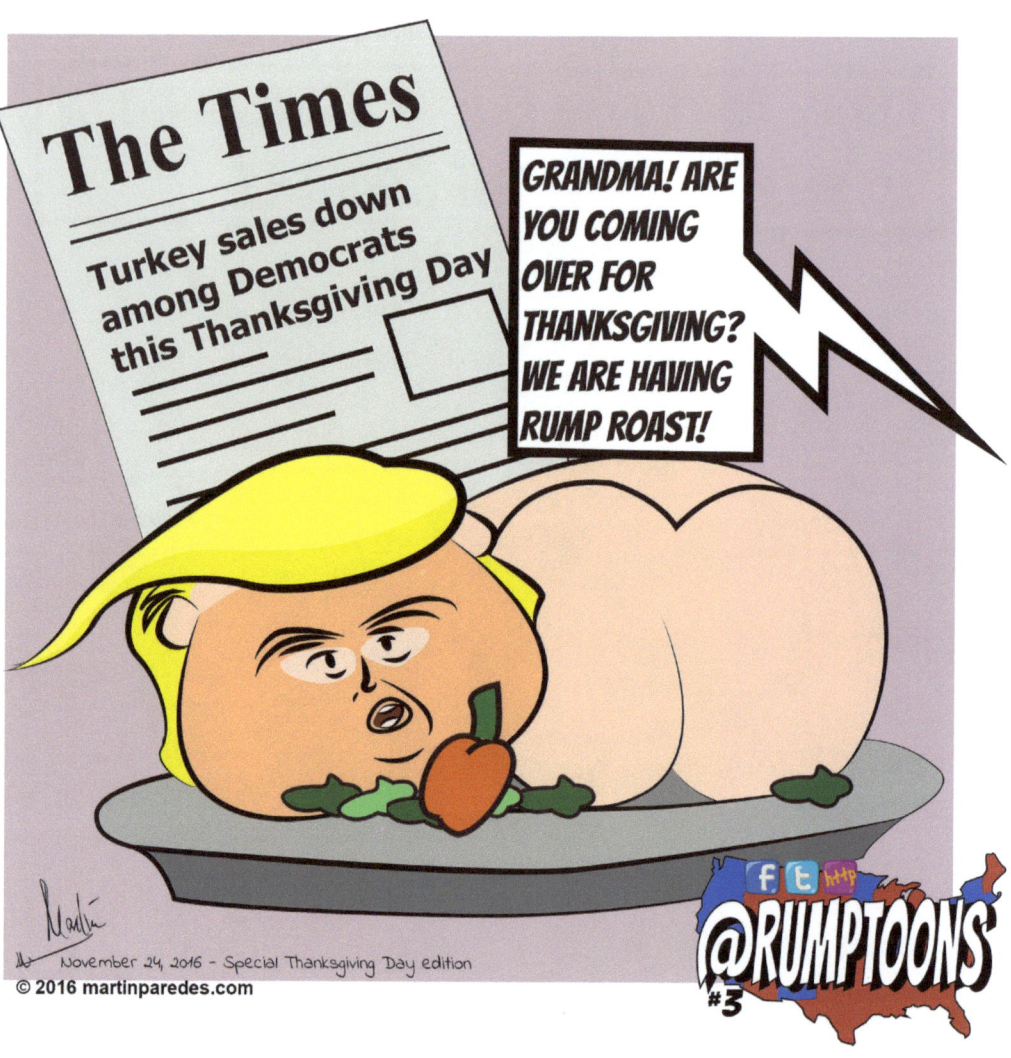

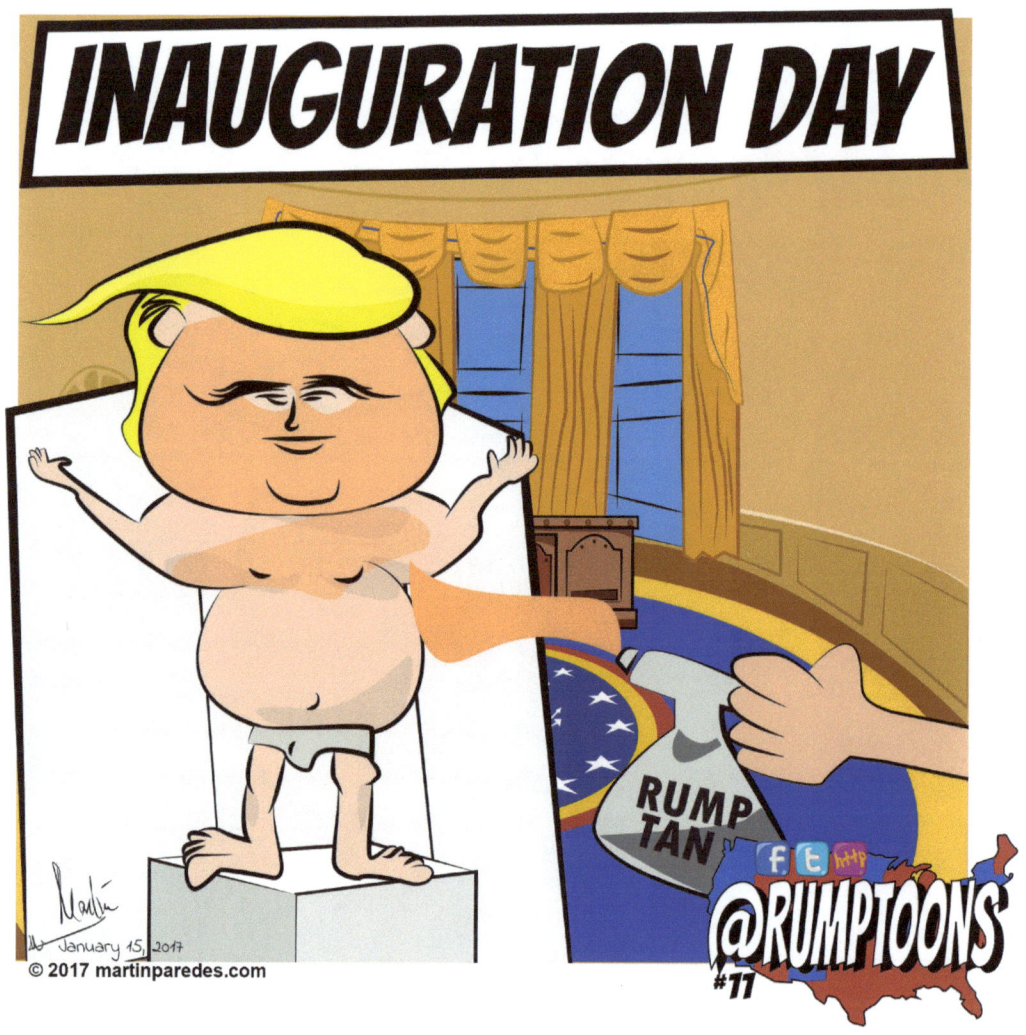

THE DONALD J TRUMP PRESIDENCY IN WEEKLY CARTOONS 2016 - 2021

RUMPTOONS

THE DONALD J TRUMP PRESIDENCY IN WEEKLY CARTOONS 2016 - 2021

RUMPTOONS

THE DONALD J TRUMP PRESIDENCY IN WEEKLY CARTOONS 2016 - 2021

RUMPTOONS

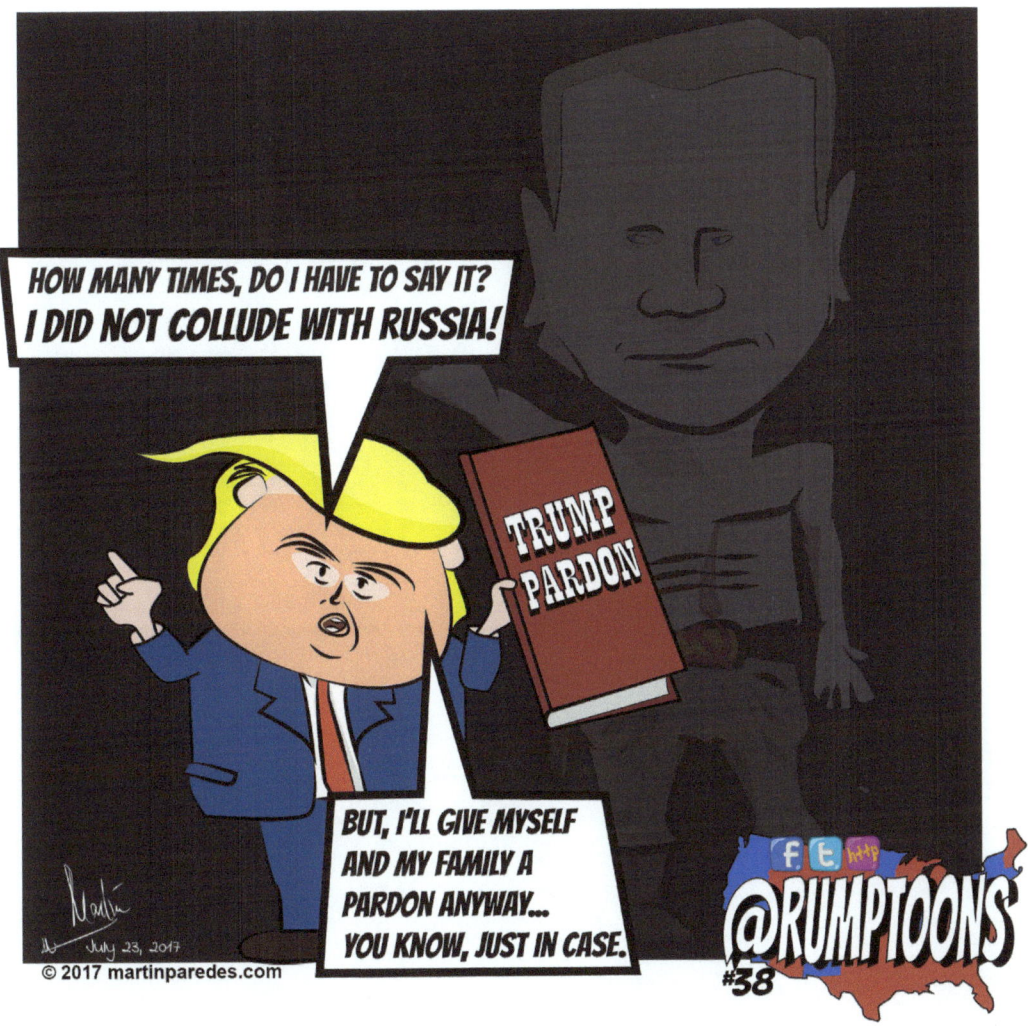

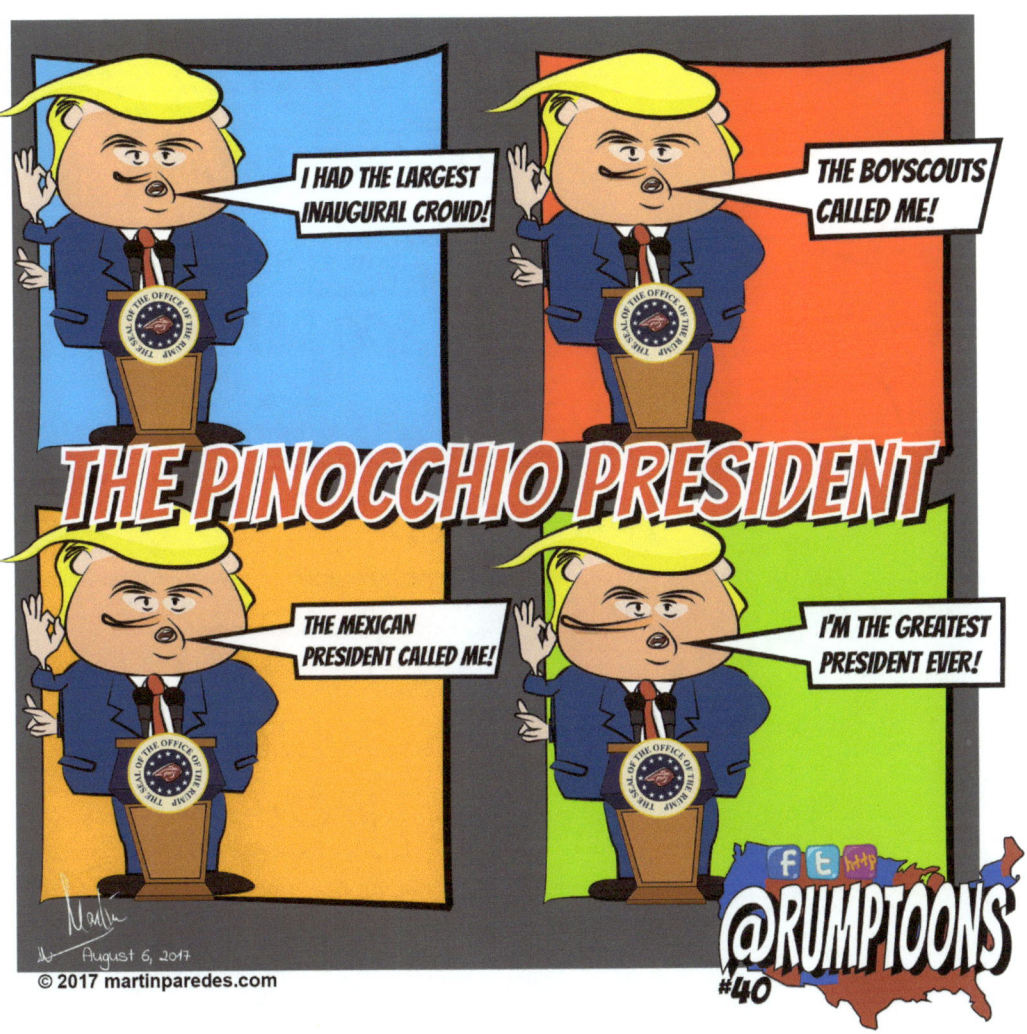

THE DONALD J TRUMP PRESIDENCY IN WEEKLY CARTOONS 2016 - 2021

THE DONALD J TRUMP PRESIDENCY IN WEEKLY CARTOONS 2016 - 2021

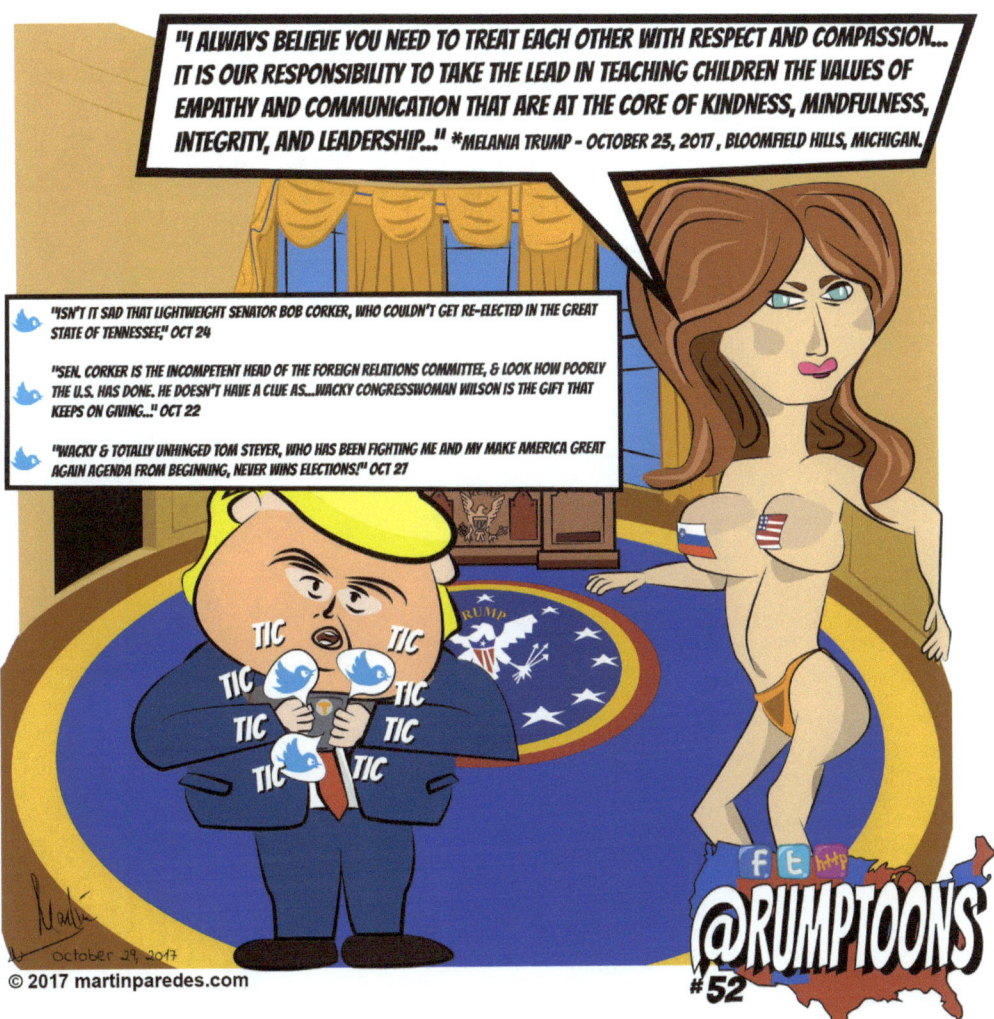

RUMPTOONS

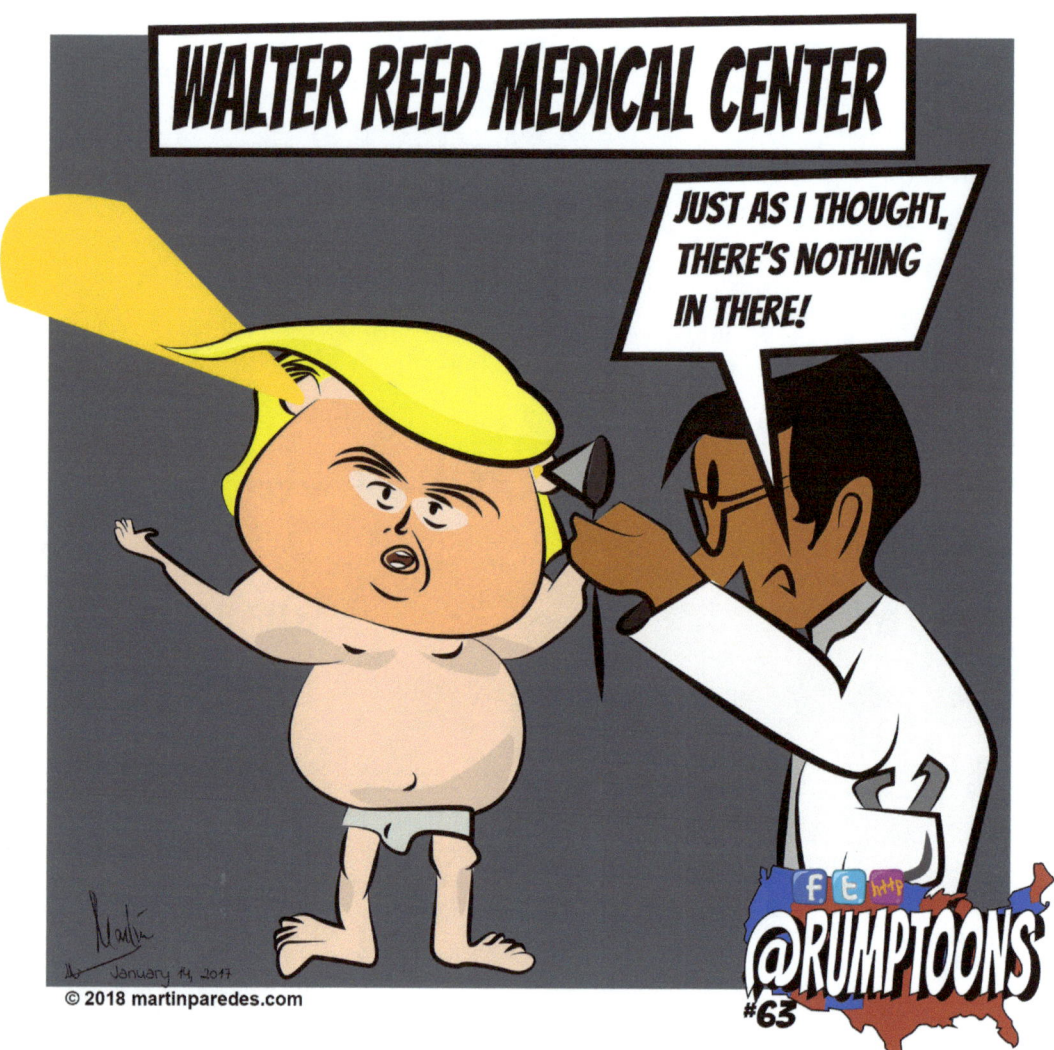

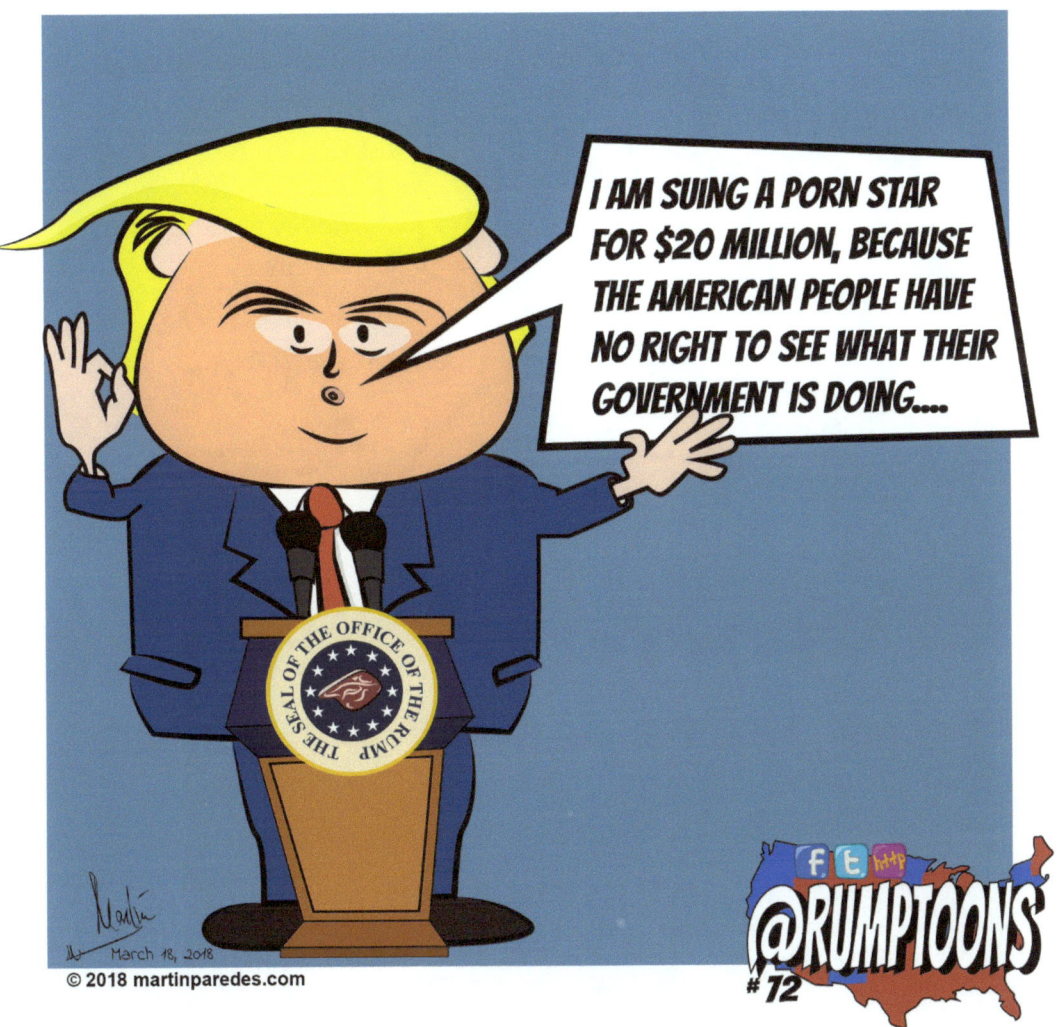

THE DONALD J TRUMP PRESIDENCY IN WEEKLY CARTOONS 2016 - 2021

RUMPTOONS

THE DONALD J TRUMP PRESIDENCY IN WEEKLY CARTOONS 2016 - 2021

RUMPTOONS

THE DONALD J TRUMP PRESIDENCY IN WEEKLY CARTOONS 2016 - 2021

RUMPTOONS

THE DONALD J TRUMP PRESIDENCY IN WEEKLY CARTOONS 2016 - 2021

THE DONALD J TRUMP PRESIDENCY IN WEEKLY CARTOONS 2016 - 2021

RUMPTOONS

THE DONALD J TRUMP PRESIDENCY IN WEEKLY CARTOONS 2016 - 2021

RUMPTOONS

THE DONALD J TRUMP PRESIDENCY IN WEEKLY CARTOONS 2016 - 2021

RUMPTOONS

THE DONALD J TRUMP PRESIDENCY IN WEEKLY CARTOONS 2016 - 2021

RUMPTOONS

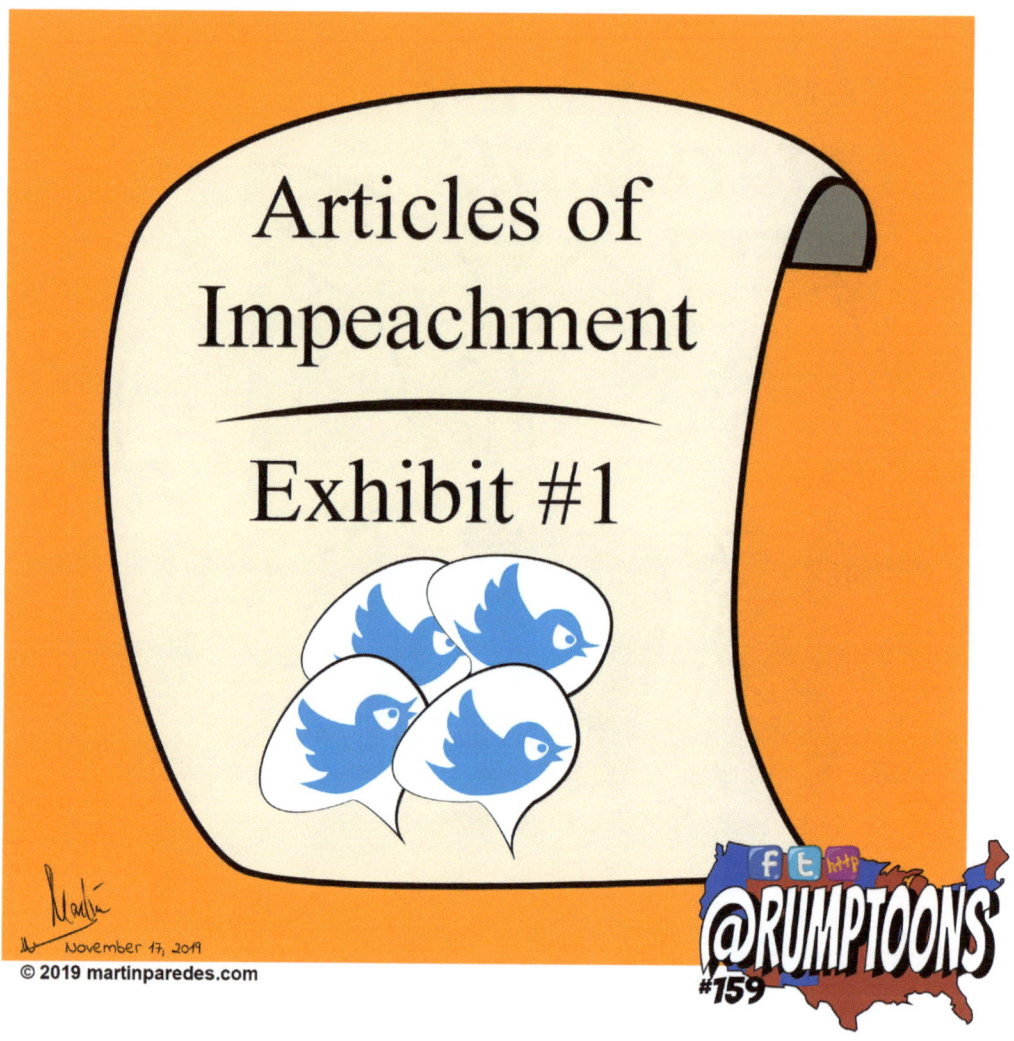

THE DONALD J TRUMP PRESIDENCY IN WEEKLY CARTOONS 2016 - 2021

THE DONALD J TRUMP PRESIDENCY IN WEEKLY CARTOONS   2016 - 2021

THE DONALD J TRUMP PRESIDENCY IN WEEKLY CARTOONS 2016 - 2021

RUMPTOONS

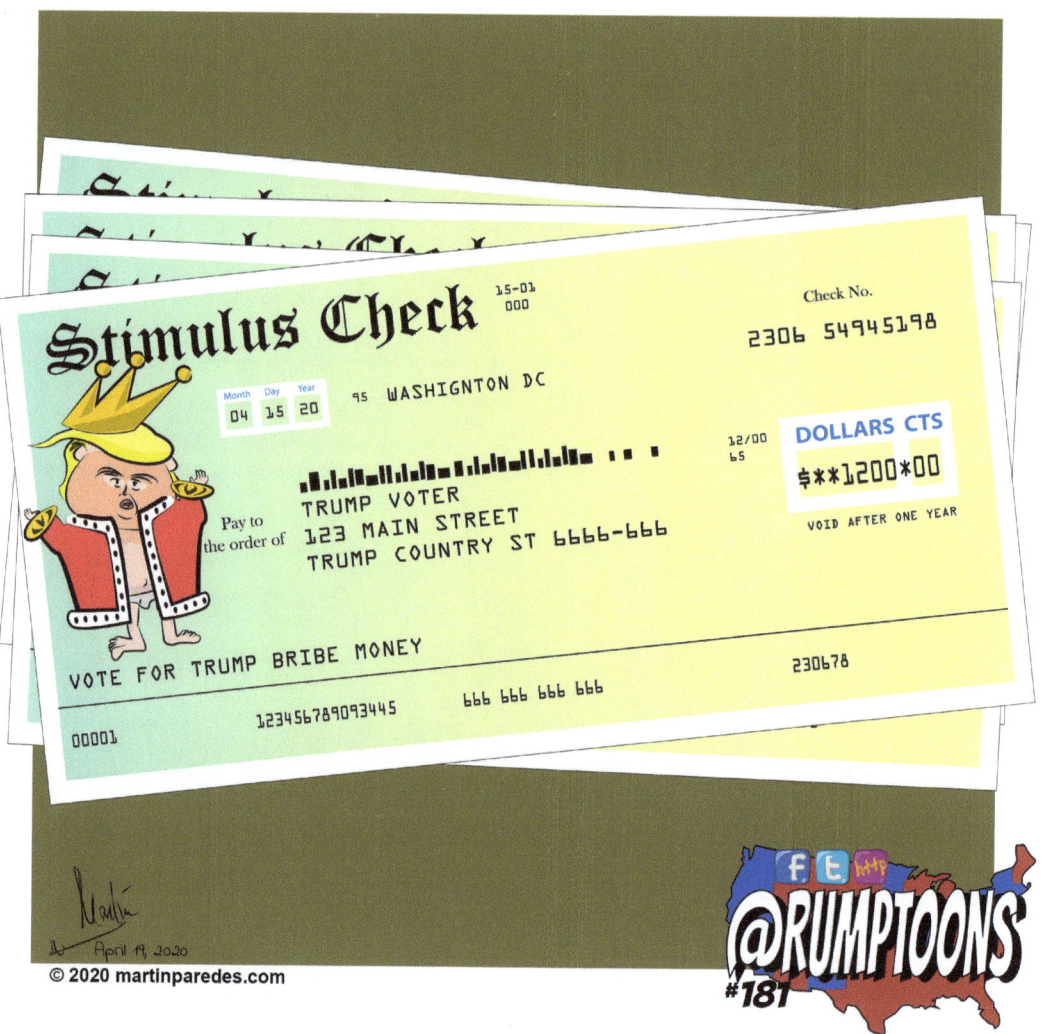

THE DONALD J TRUMP PRESIDENCY IN WEEKLY CARTOONS 2016 - 2021

RUMPTOONS

THE DONALD J TRUMP PRESIDENCY IN WEEKLY CARTOONS 2016 - 2021

RUMPTOONS

THE DONALD J TRUMP PRESIDENCY IN WEEKLY CARTOONS   2016 - 2021

THE DONALD J TRUMP PRESIDENCY IN WEEKLY CARTOONS 2016 - 2021

THE DONALD J TRUMP PRESIDENCY IN WEEKLY CARTOONS 2016 - 2021

RUMPTOONS

THE DONALD J TRUMP PRESIDENCY IN WEEKLY CARTOONS 2016 - 2021

RUMPTOONS

THE DONALD J TRUMP PRESIDENCY IN WEEKLY CARTOONS 2016 - 2021

RUMPTOONS

THE DONALD J TRUMP PRESIDENCY IN WEEKLY CARTOONS 2016 - 2021

THE DONALD J TRUMP PRESIDENCY IN WEEKLY CARTOONS 2016 - 2021

RUMPTOONS

THE DONALD J TRUMP PRESIDENCY IN WEEKLY CARTOONS 2016 - 2021

RUMPTOONS

THE DONALD J TRUMP PRESIDENCY IN WEEKLY CARTOONS 2016 - 2021

RUMPTOONS

THE DONALD J TRUMP PRESIDENCY IN WEEKLY CARTOONS 2016 - 2021

THE DONALD J TRUMP PRESIDENCY IN WEEKLY CARTOONS 2016 - 2021

Special Book Only Edition

www.ingramcontent.com/pod-product-compliance
Lightning Source LLC
Chambersburg PA
CBHW040910020526
44116CB00026B/15